# Cotton Candy

Victoria Blakemore

© 2019 Victoria Blakemore

All rights reserved. This book or parts thereof may not be reproduced in any form, stored in any retrieval system, or transmitted in any form by any means—electronic, mechanical, photocopy, recording, or otherwise—without prior written permission of the publisher, except as provided by United States of America copyright law. For permission requests, write to the publisher, at "Attention: Permissions Coordinator," at the address below.

vblakemore.author@gmail.com

Copyright info/picture credits

Cover, Brian Goodman/Shutterstock; Page 3, jack_photo/Shutterstock; Page 5, maubini/Pixabay; Page 7, Yanukit/AdobeStock; Page 9, natagolubnycha/Adobestock; Page 11, Bliss Hunter Images/Shutterstock; Page 13, Karen Shea/AdobeStock; Page 15, Voy_ager/AdobeStock; Page 17, photographyfirm/Shutterstock; Page 19, Suchart/AdobeStock; Page 21, manfredrichter/Pixabay; Page 23; Subbotina Anna/AdobeStock; Page 25, June Marie Sobrito/Shutterstock; Page 27, marioav/AdobeStock; Page 29, Bru-nO/Pixabay; Page 31, New Africa/Shutterstock; Page 32, New Africa/AdobeStock; Page 33, Brian Goodman/Shutterstock

# Table of Contents

What is Cotton Candy?     2

Ingredients     4

Flavors     6

History     8

Making Cotton Candy     12

Spun Sugar     16

Cotton Candy Around the World     18

Cotton Candy Grapes     20

Cotton Candy in Other Foods     22

Carnivals     24

Cotton Candy Day     26

Nutrition     28

Cotton Candy at Home     30

Glossary     34

# What is Cotton Candy?

Cotton candy is a sweet treat often sold at carnivals and fairs. It gets its name from the way the **strands** of sugar are similar to cotton.

Cotton candy has a few different names. In England, it is called candy floss. In Australia, it is called fairy floss.

In the Netherlands, cotton candy is called **suikerspin**, which means "sugar spider."

# Ingredients

Cotton candy can be made with only one ingredient. That ingredient is sugar. When made with only sugar, cotton candy is white and sweet.

Candy flavorings can also be added to the cotton candy to change the flavor.

Food color or **dye** is usually added to cotton candy. It is most often made with pink, blue, or yellow.

# Flavors

Most cotton candy just has a sweet taste. Liquid or powdered flavorings can be added to the sugar to change the flavor.

Cotton candy can be flavored to be like fruits, foods, drinks, or other candies. Some flavorings also change the color of the cotton candy.

Popular cotton candy flavors include bubblegum, raspberry, and watermelon.

# History

Cotton candy as we know it was first made in 1899. John C. Wharton, a candy maker, and William J. Morrison, a dentist worked together to make a candy machine.

Their machine was able to spin melted sugar into **strands**. This used to be done by hand.

The two inventors called their spun sugar "fairy floss" because it was so light and airy.

In 1904, cotton candy was sold at the St. Louis World's Fair. It was sold for twenty-five cents for a box. It was very popular and sold over $17,000 in six months.

The first cotton candy machines broke down a lot. They have been **improved** in the years since they were created.

In 1972, the first **automated** cotton candy machine was created. It is able to run without help from people.

# Making Cotton Candy

There are two kinds of machines that make cotton candy. One works without human help. It is used to make large amounts of cotton candy for sale in stores.

The other machine is often used at carnivals and festivals. It makes smaller amounts of cotton candy at a time.

Both machines start by heating sugar until it melts. The sugar is spun until it comes out in long **strands.**

In the larger machines, the **strands** are put together to make a large bundle. They are then packaged for sale.

In the machines used at carnivals, the person running the machine collects the sugar **strands**. They often use a cone or tube to collect the sugar.

When the **strands** of sugar are put together, air gets trapped among them. This makes cotton candy light and fluffy.

# Spun Sugar

Before there was cotton candy, there was spun sugar. It was made hundreds of years ago in parts of Europe and Asia.

Spun sugar is made by melting sugar into a liquid. The liquid is drizzled into **strands**. The **strands** can be made into different shapes.

Spun sugar is often used to decorate desserts like cupcakes, cakes, and fruit tarts.

# Cotton Candy Around the World

Cotton candy is enjoyed by people all over the world. In China, sugar **strands** are stretched out to make a treat called dragon's beard.

In Turkey, a treat called keten helva is made by roasting flour in butter, then adding pulled sugar.

Roti sai mai is a treat made in Thailand. It is made by wrapping cotton candy in a thin, sweet crepe.

# Cotton Candy Grapes

Scientists have created grapes that taste like cotton candy. They were created by combining two different kinds of grapes.

The cotton candy grapes do not have the tartness found in other grapes. This allows their sweet taste to be more **potent**.

Cotton candy grapes look like regular green grapes, but they are much sweeter.

# Cotton Candy in Other Foods

Cotton candy and cotton candy flavoring can be added to many other foods.

It is sometimes used to top other treats such as donuts or ice cream. It can also be used to create new treats. Ice cream burritos can be made using cotton candy as the wrapping.

Cotton candy flavoring is often added to treats like ice cream.

23

# Carnivals

Cotton candy is a popular treat at carnivals, circuses, and fairs. It has been this way since it was first introduced at the World's Fair in 1904.

Some cotton candy machines are on carts that can be moved around the fair. Others are inside food trucks.

Cotton candy is often sold alongside other treats such as candy apples and popcorn.

# Cotton Candy Day

There are two days for celebrating cotton candy. Cotton candy day is on July 31st and also on December 7th.

Some people celebrate cotton candy day by buying or making cotton candy.

# Nutrition

Cotton candy is made up entirely of sugar. All of the **calories** in cotton candy are from the sugar.

It doesn't contain any vitamins or other nutrients that our bodies need. It is simply a sweet treat.

Cotton candy should be eaten in **moderation**. Too much sugar isn't good for you.

# Cotton Candy at Home

Cotton candy doesn't have to be just for carnivals and fairs. It can also be made and enjoyed at home.

Some people make spun or pulled sugar by hand. It isn't usually eaten on its own like cotton candy, but it is similar.

Some companies have cotton candy machines for making your own cotton candy at home.

Home cotton candy machines can be used to make cotton candy treats for parties.

# Glossary

**Automated**: able to run by mechanical means, without human help

**Calories**: units for measuring the amount of energy a food can make when taken in by the body

**Dye**: a substance used to give color to cloth, food, or hair

**Improved**: made better

**Moderation**: not having too much

**Potent**: having strength, powerful

**Strands**: lengths of fibers, strings

**Suikerspin**: the name for a cotton candy treat enjoyed in the Netherlands, "sugar spider"

# About the Author

Victoria Blakemore is a first grade teacher in Southwest Florida with a passion for reading.

You can visit her at

www.elementaryexplorers.com

# Also in This Series

# Also in This Series

www.ingramcontent.com/pod-product-compliance
Lightning Source LLC
Chambersburg PA
CBHW041321110526
44591CB00021B/2869